CW01512591

Original title:
Bracelets for the Brave

Author: Levi Montgomery
ISBN HARDBACK: 978-1-80586-035-8
ISBN PAPERBACK: 978-1-80586-507-0

Emblems of Strength

On my wrist, a rubber band,
It holds my hopes, it makes me stand.
With every twist, a little cheer,
I'm strong as steel, or maybe beer!

A charm that jingles when I dance,
It tells the world, I take a chance.
Each bead's a tale of laughs and tears,
A fashion statement, don't you sneers!

Tokens of Triumph

This little loop of sparkly gold,
Reminds me of adventures bold.
With every turn, a funny tale,
Like when I tripped and almost fell!

A charm with laughter, joy, and jest,
It keeps my spirits at their best.
Each color shines, a memory bright,
Worn on adventures day or night!

Weaving Hope into Armlets

Look at my wrist, a rainbow feast,
With silly shapes, it breaks the least.
A unicorn, a pie, a cat!
What hope lies there, imagine that!

Each twist, a laugh, a happy dance,
These silly charms just take a chance.
They jingle-jangle through the day,
And keep the blues so far away!

Symbols of Grit

My wrist is wrapped in colors bright,
A symbol of my silly fight.
With every twist, I roll my sleeves,
And conquer doubts that life retrieves!

These tokens silly, not so tough,
With wiggly worms, they look quite buff.
They cheer me on with every guest,
In this wild life, I'm truly blessed!

Talismans of Spirit

A band of color wrapped so tight,
With charms that jingle, oh what a sight!
They say it brings luck, or a giggle or two,
Worn by the fearless, and sometimes the blue.

On wrists they dance, in sunlight they play,
Tickling the brave on a hard-working day.
With stories to tell, and laughs to impart,
Each twist and turn, a wobbly art.

So slap one on, join the playful parade,
Join the mischief, don't be afraid!
These colorful loops are more than they seem,
Naughty reminders of fun in a dream.

So here's to the bands, both silly and bold,
With hearts made of laughter and tales yet untold.
In every ding and jingle, find joy to embrace,
For every brave wearer, there's a smile on their face.

Legacy of Bravery

Worn like armor, a badge of pride,
Each jangly piece has a story inside.
From grand tales of battle to antics absurd,
These lively mementos are anything but blurred.

Fingers twist 'round them, a blessing of sorts,
Who knew that courage could have such support?
They clink and they clatter, a rhythm of cheer,
Even the bravest need giggles, it's clear!

Like knights in bright colors, conquering fears,
They laugh in the face of doubt and of sneers.
With a wink and a grin, they spread joy with flair,
These whimsical wonders, bold souls declare!

Lost in the laughter, the tales intertwine,
Of hiccups and tumbles, oh ain't it divine!
So wear them with honor, these spirited bands,
For bravery's legacy is in all of our hands.

Crafting Courage

Snipping and snazzing, with glitter and glue,
We make them a style you just can't subdue.
A dash of this, and a pinch of that,
For every brave heart that laughs like a cat.

Threading together our fanciful dreams,
In colors that pop, with sly little gleams.
With tools of fun, we craft and we cheer,
Who knew that courage could tickle the ear?

A tug here and there, oh what a surprise,
As whimsy and boldness bring chuckles and sighs.
From the tip of a laugh to the roll of a smile,
We gather the brave, let's hang for a while!

So join in the fun, grab scissors and lace,
We're crafting some courage, let's fill up the space!
These joyful creations will always be found,
On the arms of the brave, where laughter abounds.

Stories in Chains

In tangled tales, where laughter's the key,
We wear our histories, wild and free.
A chain of giggles, a loop of delight,
Intertwined moments, shining so bright.

Each link holds a secret, a mischief or two,
Of daring adventures and friendships tried true.
They jingle and jangle, like whispers of cheer,
With a leaf of a giggle, they draw us near.

So clasp those odd bits, don't let them fade,
For every brave soul has mischief displayed.
With colorful stories wrapped round our wrist,
Join the carnival, you'd never want missed!

In chains of jest, where memories laugh,
Each piece spins a yarn, like a joyous craft.
For the brave wear these tales, with humor, they cheer,
In this whimsical world, let's spread all the cheer!

Artifacts of the Stalwart

In a world of tasks, so bold and outlandish,
They wear colorful bands, quite simply Manish.
Tales of heroism, in colors so bright,
Yet the dog ate them all, what a comical plight!

Crafted by hands, but lost in the fray,
They juggle their duties in a whimsical way.
With each little mishap, a chuckle they share,
Who knew being brave could lead to such flair?

A flick of the wrist, and off they go,
To save the day with a colorful show.
Adventures await, with laughter and cheer,
Their artifacts gleam, but let's not mention near!

So if you happen to spot a rogue thread,
That once was a symbol of deeds widely spread,
Just smile and remember the joy they instill,
In a silly charade of courage and thrill.

Pendants of Perseverance

They hang from their necks, like medals of jest,
Pieces of humor, a quirky contest.
Each pendant a story, some silly, some bright,
Like the time they tripped over their own shoe's might!

In battle they stand, with laughter their shield,
Facing the day while their memories yield.
Do they swing in tension, or dance with delight?
These trinkets of pluck keep them light as a kite!

Each swing tells a tale of mishaps and glee,
While wading through puddles, oh what a spree!
A reminder perhaps, that bravery's fun,
With quirky adornments, their worries undone.

So join in the laughter, extend your good cheer,
For every victorious triumph holds dear.
Their pendants will shimmer and twirl with a grin,
In a whimsical world where laughter can win!

Spheres of Strength

Round little baubles, they perfect the art,
Of juggling their woes with a light-hearted start.
Each sphere a reminder of things that they face,
Like the time they sneezed all over the place!

Gloriously rolling through life's funny scene,
With dazzling resilience dancing in between.
They bounce with such flair, akin to a ball,
Hurdling their worries, and laughing through it all!

A toss of their spirit, and watch them defy,
The everyday troubles which seem to supply.
Each sphere tells a joke that no one can miss,
Like the time they slipped and fell in pure bliss!

So here's to the bouncers of life's crazy game,
With spheres of pure strength, they're never the same.
Adding fun to the fight, with a giggle or cheer,
Their joy is infectious, they spread far and near!

Treasures of the Determined

Hidden in pockets, in bags worn with flair,
Lay treasures of grit, sprinkled everywhere.
Each trinket a gem from life's rugged terrain,
Like the time they forgot where they left their train!

Wrapped in their journeys, their heartbeats collide,
With laughter that sparkles, and joy they can't hide.
No burden too heavy, no frown they see,
As they trip on the path to what's truly free!

With every treasure, a story unfolds,
Of epic misadventures, both brave and bold.
The world may be wacky, but together they stand,
In a circus of courage, they'll make life so grand!

So lift up your treasures, let laughter ignite,
For determined folks shine like stars in the night.
In a world full of whimsy, they joyfully tread,
With a cackle of laughter that no one can shred!

Expressions of Courage

In a world where courage wears a smile,
Heroes come in colorful styles.
With charms that jingle and beads that glow,
They strut their stuff, putting on a show.

Some wear stars, others wear pride,
A funky flair, a bright blue tide.
With laughter loud and hearts so free,
These silly symbols, oh can't you see?

They dance through life, like pets on a leash,
Unfurling joy, like a circus beast.
With winks and nods, they play the part,
In rubber and thread, they wear their heart.

So here's to the brave in vivid attire,
Who lighten the load and spark the fire.
With a twist and a twirl, they'll always find,
Life's an adventure for the fun-loving kind.

Harmonies of the Brave

In the concert of courage, they strum away,
Making music with laughter, come join the play.
With jingles that sparkle, a rhythmic cheer,
Their tales of valor are joyfully clear.

Each bead a note, each charm a song,
In this quirky symphony, you can't go wrong.
With moonlit laughter and sun-kissed thrills,
They turn fears to giggles, and heartaches to spills.

From the quiet to the loud, they sing their tune,
With disco lights flashing, under the moon.
In the choir of courage, they dance and prance,
Painting smiles on faces with each reckless chance.

So raise your glass to the jesters of fate,
Who remind us all to celebrate!
With harmonies bright and rhythms to sway,
Life's better together, come join the fray!

Wreaths of Resolve

In gardens of grit, they spiral and twirl,
Crafting wreaths of resolve, they give courage a whirl.
With petals of laughter, stitched with esteem,
They bloom where they're planted, living the dream.

Twisted with flair, adorned with a smile,
Their antics are treasures that stretch for a mile.
With colors so vivid, they weave a delight,
Turning mundane moments into sheer delight.

Their stories unfurl like ribbons on trees,
Tickling the heart, putting doubts at ease.
In the shade of tough times, they stand so bold,
With a wink and a laugh, their joy's pure gold.

So wrap yourself tight in these threads of cheer,
With wreaths of resolve, there's nothing to fear.
Together we flourish, like flowers in sun,
With joy as our armor, we rise up as one.

Heartfelt Reminders

In the little moments, we find our way,
With hints of adventure to brighten the day.
These charming reminders, as light as a feather,
Bring warmth to the heart, let's tether together.

From the tickles of friendship to giggles we share,
Every trinket holds memories, light as air.
Crafting bonds stronger with laughter we lace,
In this quirky dance, we find our place.

The silly stories we tell, the fun that we weave,
Are heartfelt reminders of what we believe.
With quirky little symbols, we strut through the night,
With courage and humor, we're shining so bright.

So here's to the brave with sparks in their gaze,
Ensuring each moment's a whimsical blaze.
With laughter our language, we boldly declare,
Life's a silly dance, so come join the fair!

Inspirations in Metal

In a world of shiny charms,
Where quirks and laughter dwell,
Worn by those with hidden harms,
Each clasp holds a tale to tell.

They jingle like a joyful band,
Each twist and turn absurd,
Adventures nearly unplanned,
With every clink, a laugh is heard.

They shine through every smile,
In colors bold and bright,
Funny faces all the while,
Dancing in the light.

So if you find a sparkly chain,
With whimsy for your wrist,
Just know it holds a bit of pain,
And also, joy is kissed!

Heirlooms of Audacity

A treasure passed from hand to hand,
With stories ripe and rare,
Each piece a bold and crazy brand,
Of courage, laughs, and flair.

In Grandma's drawer, a wild find,
A loop that makes us grin,
Silly shapes and colors combined,
Adventure wrapped in tin.

Worn during moments of great glee,
Or times when fears arise,
These trinkets beam with certainty,
And twinkle like the skies.

In every clink, a silly cheer,
In every twist, a spark,
Heirlooms glorious, loud, and clear,
Become our truth, our lark!

Souvenirs of the Unfazed

Traveling far with quirky goods,
From markets and from fairs,
With pieces from the strangest woods,
That tickle at our cares.

Potato smiles and unicorns,
What treasures do they hold?
Each laugh, a shield against the scorns,
In our hearts, pure gold.

They jingle as we twirl around,
A merry little song,
In colors bright, they spread the sound,
Of laughter all day long.

So let's embrace these gifts of cheer,
As whimsies take their place,
For every shake, a truth is clear,
In joyful, silly grace!

Relics of Resilience

Oh, what tales these trinkets spin,
Of moments gone astray,
They wear their scars like a badge of win,
And laugh at life's ballet.

A nod to risks we dared to take,
With beads of humor bright,
Each failure's just a giggle quake,
In relentless, joyful fight.

These tokens of our silly past,
Glimmer in the sun,
Each memory designed to last,
In laughter, we have won.

So clasp them on with all your might,
And strut through life with flair,
For every wink and every bite,
Leaves riddles in the air!

Custom Threads of Tenacity

In a world of yarn and string,
We craft our tales with little bling.
With knots that hold our dreams in place,
And colors bright, we share a space.

A tangled mess, yet oh so neat,
We wear our battles, can't be beat.
Each twist and turn a story told,
Of laughter, courage, hearts of gold.

So gather 'round, let's tie a strand,
With threads of hope, we make a stand.
A jolly crew, we flick our wrists,
With custom threads, we can't resist.

Armor for the Heart

In life's wild circus, here we are,
Wearing our trinkets like a star.
With charms that jingle, spirits rise,
We dance through storms, oh what a prize!

From glitter glue to sparkly glue,
Our armor shines, it's tried and true.
When laughter strikes and troubles loom,
We twirl and glide, dispelling gloom.

So raise your wrist, let's take a chance,
In this crazy, zany, dance!
With hearts so bold and minds so smart,
We wear our love, our shield, our heart.

Strands of Honor

In the land of friendship, where we play,
Strands of honor cheer the day.
With colors like the rainbow bright,
We weave together, pure delight.

Each loop a laugh, each knot a cheer,
Binding us close, year after year.
With silly faces, we strut and sway,
In strands of honor, let's have a play!

Our memories cling, like glue they stay,
Through thick and thin, come what may.
With quirky charms and stories grand,
We twirl in circles, hand in hand.

Mementos of the Indomitable

Through trials faced with humor bright,
We wear our mementos, a comical sight.
Each charm a giggle, a memory sweet,
The battles fought and still on our feet.

In wacky shapes, our pride we flaunt,
With every twist, a joyful taunt.
For life is but a funny game,
With laughter woven in our name.

So clasp your gift of silly flair,
In mementos bold, we light the air.
Together we shine, a whimsical team,
In every strand, a joyful dream.

Woven Dreams of Valor

In a world where cowboys dance,
A hero puts on their silly pants.
With beads that jingle, they do twirl,
Saving kittens, watch them whirl.

They wear their charms, not on the wrist,
Each one with a secret twist.
Laughter echoes in the sky,
As capes are swapped for donuts, oh my!

Each thread a tale of goofy fights,
With gummy bears and disco lights.
When danger calls, they just might jest,
And leave the villains quite distressed.

So grab your charm, take up the cause,
With silly symbols, just because.
In every giggle, there they stand,
Linking hearts across the land.

Signets of Heroism

With a ring that shines and puffed-up chest,
A hero claims their silly quest.
Waving a foam finger high,
Pretending to soar through the pie in the sky.

These signets tell of brave misdeeds,
Like fighting dragons made of beads.
They trip on capes and land in mud,
But laugh it off with a playful thud.

Their armor made of rainbow socks,
They hoard their snacks like treasure boxes.
Defending snacks from all the foes,
With jellybeans ready for a pose!

A hero's pride, in colors bright,
Dancing silly 'neath golden light.
In every chuckle, courage lives,
With a light heart, true grit it gives.

Beads of Bravery

With beads strung up like stories told,
Each one shines with bravery bold.
A mismatched lot, they laugh and sing,
In battles fierce with… ping-pong balls fling!

These tiny gems of goofy tales,
Stand guard against the silliest gales.
Launching pies with all their might,
They brave the chaos, hearts in flight.

Every bead holds a funny stunt,
A hero's laugh, they're on the hunt.
Saving the day with tickles galore,
In a world where giggles soar.

So string them on, let courage flow,
With every bead, let your smile grow.
For in this crazy, laughter's key,
Is the bravest heart that's wild and free!

Threads of Grit

With threads so bright, they twist and twine,
A hero's garb, an outfit divine.
Stitching laughter into each hole,
Embroidering joy, they take their toll.

They leap and bound, in threads of cheer,
Fighting gloom with a hearty jeer.
With lollipop swords, they draw a line,
And dance around, feeling just fine.

In wacky capes, adorned in flair,
No daring deed too tough to bear.
Each step a kick, each fall a race,
For funny heroes, it's just a chase.

So wrap your wrist in magic thread,
With tales of joy in all you spread.
For the boldest hearts wear laughter's kit,
In threads of grit, they joyfully sit.

Threads of Courage

In a land where socks do roam,
Brave souls wear threads as their home.
They twirl and dance with flair and zest,
Making every heart feel blessed.

With colors bright and patterns wild,
They laugh and joke like a carefree child.
Each twist and turn brings giggles galore,
Courage weaves in every score.

When the sun is hot, and the sweat does flow,
These threads hug tight, stealing the show.
With styles bold and puns on cue,
Every glance turns a frown to woo.

So raise a toast to threads of cheer,
Crafted with love, let's make it clear.
For when the world feels a little tough,
We wear our colors, that's just enough.

Adornments of Valor

A shiny trinket and a wink so sly,
Add some flair and soar up high.
With charm and giggle, we strut our stuff,
Making the mundane just a bit more tough.

Dangle a bauble, swap a smile,
These adornments make the world worthwhile.
They tinkle and jingle, oh what a show,
Showcasing courage wherever we go.

When life gets heavy, glimmer and shine,
With every twirl, we continue to dine.
Laughing at trials, like a dance on air,
Valor shines brighter, showing we care.

So stack those gems, don't be too shy,
In a world of chaos, let your spirit fly.
For with each sparkle, we create our tale,
In joy and honor, together we sail.

The Band of Resilience

A funky crew, we wear our pride,
Resilience festooned right at our sides.
With colorful flair and silly hats,
We scheme and dream, just like cool cats.

When troubles come knocking, we laugh and cheer,
With a band of mates, there's nothing to fear.
We jive and we shimmy, no chore's too rough,
Resilient hearts are made of tough stuff.

With each wild twirl and goofy dance,
We sprout like daisies, given the chance.
Strung together like notes in a song,
United we claim, nothing's ever wrong.

So join the band, let's make some noise,
In this wacky crew, we find our joys.
For in every twist and every spin,
Resilience is where the fun begins!

Charms of the Fearless

Oh, the charms that dangle and shine,
Fearless spirits, oh how they combine!
With giggles and glimmers, we craft our dreams,
Dancing through life, bursting at the seams.

A sprinkle of fun, a dash of cheek,
These charms bring laughter, making us unique.
When worries rise like a pesky foe,
Fearless hearts shine bright like a show.

They jingle with joy, telling stories bold,
Of mishaps and triumphs, that's how we're sold.
A flick of the wrist, a wink of an eye,
Fearless together, we touch the sky.

So let's adorn ourselves with quirky guise,
In the face of adventure, we'll always rise.
For in every charm, and in every jest,
Fearlessness lives, and we feel blessed.

Courage in Chains

A warrior's wrist, adorned with flair,
Jokes on tension, wear and tear.
A trinket shines, so bright and merry,
Who knew bravery could be so hairy?

Each charm a tale, a laugh to share,
Fighting fears with flair and care.
Dare you dangle, dodge the doubt?
Or just wear these gems, that's what they're about!

Tangled threads of bold delight,
Giggles echo through the night.
When battles seem to drag you down,
Wear your bling and hoist a crown!

So if you're brave, just flash that style,
Kick fear aside with grace and guile.
Embrace the whimsy, sail the seas,
With funky beads that bring the peace!

Spirals of Strength

Around the wrist, such colors spin,
Each layer whispers, "Let's begin!"
In circles bright, they twist and weave,
Stand tall with laughs, you won't believe!

The spiral dance, so wild and free,
Cracks a smile, simple as can be.
When courage gets a little stale,
Just look at your wrist—it'll never fail!

Each turn a story, each twist a pun,
Making fun of fears, while on the run.
Who'd have thought such bling could teach,
Strength comes wrapped, right at your reach?

So when life's chaos gets in your face,
Remember your wrists, and find your place.
With every spiral, every twinkling chance,
Laugh through the fear, put on your dance!

Fenestrations of Hope

Through the gaps of doubt and strife,
Shine small windows, light and life.
A little glimmer, a touch of glee,
Wearing dreams like a bright marquee.

Each bead a window, peeking through,
Surprising truths, like morning dew.
With every glance, a chuckle bound,
In the light of humor, strength is found.

Hope's a locket, flapping wide,
Not locked away, but a seaside ride.
When things get tough, just give a wink,
Your wrist is magic; just stop and think!

So laugh at shadows that loom so near,
Each little charm chases off the fear.
In this whimsical dance of fate,
With open windows, we celebrate!

Tapestry of the Fearless

Threads of courage, bright and bold,
Stitching smiles as stories unfold.
With every charm, a snicker shared,
From fierce to funny — we're all impaired!

A tapestry woven, wild and grand,
Life's funny moments, we've all planned.
Fears might loom, like monsters in beds,
But we've got laughter, tying our threads!

Every knot a giggle, every weave a cheer,
A colorful shield against the sneer.
When courage falters, just look inside,
This tapestry holds every silly ride.

So join the dance, with beads ablaze,
Laugh at fears, in whimsical ways.
With every wrap of this merry spin,
We're all the fearless, let the fun begin!

Emblems of Strength

A shiny charm, oh what a sight,
It jingles with all its might.
Yet when I wave, it flies away,
A peekaboo game, come out to play!

In meetings, clinks make me a star,
While secretly hiding snack from afar.
The sparkle shines, but wait a tick,
What's that? Oh no! It's stuck to my mic!

Each color tells a silly tale,
Of failed attempts in the grocery trail.
Hey, look at me, with pride I wear,
My multi-hued, not-so-secret share!

When chores are done and vibes are right,
I wear my charms, feeling light.
For laughter's found in every twist,
An emblem of strength in my wrist's fist!

Bangles of the Fearless

On my wrist, they dance and jive,
Making sure I feel alive.
Each bang a note of glee and fun,
Reminding me of battles won!

I slide them on, they cling and cling,
Like pesky bugs in early spring.
Yet when I run, they bounce and shake,
Falling off like a funny mistake!

When I wave, they waltz and flee,
Chasing down the cat, oh silly spree!
A circus act in the living room,
My bangles bring on all the zoom!

To the brave they are sworn,
But on my wrist, they've been reborn.
With each playful twist and cheer,
They spread the joy, bringing near!

Tokens of Resolve

Tiny trinkets wrap around tight,
Assuring me I'll win the fight.
Though sometimes they can be a fool,
For sneaking snacks is their main rule!

Donning these gifts from a distant friend,
I giggle at their clumsy blend.
With every jingle, they start to sway,
As if to say, 'Let's seize the day!'

Each color shines, a tale to tell,
Of mishaps shared, oh so well.
A pop of humor, a dash of pride,
These tokens are my joy worldwide!

When challenges rise, I'll wear them bright,
And face the world with all my might.
With laughter armed and wit in hand,
These tokens ensure I'll stand grand!

Armlets of the Audacious

With armlets snug against my skin,
I'm ready for the games to begin.
But as I chase, they fly and dive,
A comedic twist, oh how they thrive!

Each one tells a tale of bold,
Of moments wild, both new and old.
As I strut with a swagger, watch them swirl,
A carnival of giggles, oh what a whirl!

In the mirror, I pose with flair,
But wave goodbye to my goofy pair.
They tumble down, a clattering sound,
While laughter echoes all around!

Ode to the brave, and jesters too,
With audacity, my dreams come true.
An armlet cheer for the joyful chase,
With each slip-up, I still embrace!

Adornments of the Undaunted

A shiny band on every wrist,
Says 'I'm here, I do exist!'
With charms that jingle, all in place,
They dance around, a cheerful race.

Each one tells tales of quirky deeds,
Like fearless cats and valiant steeds.
They laugh and twirl, oh what a sight,
Adornments bright in morning light.

Some twist and shout, some softly gleam,
They know they're part of every dream.
With colors bold, they make a scene,
Adventures shared, Oh, what a team!

So wear them proud, don't be dismayed,
These little gems, an amusing trade.
For in each glimmer, laughter sprouts,
All for the brave, without a doubt!

Links of Fortitude

These links of strength, a silly game,
With every clasp, you shout my name!
Some are floppy, some are tight,
Jingling joy, oh what a sight!

They wiggle now, they jiggle then,
Chasing courage through the glen.
Wear them bold, wear them loud,
In every room, we'll draw a crowd!

A pirate's hook, a funky star,
With goofy charms from near and far.
They dangle dreams of all the fun,
Linked in laughter, everyone!

So strap them on, let voices rise,
For every wearer, a surprise.
In silly moments, hearts embrace,
Links of courage, the brave in place!

Jewelry of the Intrepid

Dazzling rocks that tell their tale,
Of fearless hearts that will not pale.
A bracelet here, a pendant there,
They shimmer bright, the joy we share.

With beads that wiggle and pendants swing,
Where strength of spirit makes us sing.
Each stitch of laughter, woven in,
Jewelry that makes the boldest grin!

There's sparkle fierce and glitter shy,
Adventures waiting in the sky.
Put them on and do a dance,
This is our moment, take a chance!

So here we stand, a motley crew,
With silly gems, we'll break right through.
In every clasp, a little cheer,
Wear this joy, let go your fear!

Accolades of the Fearless

A clap of colors wraps the wrist,
With awards for those who dare to twist.
Each charm a shout of victory bright,
For those who laugh in face of fright.

They shimmer bold like a brave parade,
Accolades for jokes we've made.
From silly pranks to daring stunts,
These trinkets shine, oh how it fronts!

Together we stand, a goofy swarm,
Each bracelet buzzing, weathering storm.
Trinkets twinkle, stories to tell,
Fearless hearts, we wear them well!

So gather round, let's raise a cheer,
With accolades that bring us near.
These tokens laugh at all we've faced,
For every brave soul, a trinket graced!

Wares of the Fearless Heart

On the wrist, a token shines,
Wrapped around with jokes and lines.
A charm for every silly feat,
It squeaks a laugh with every beat.

Ready to tackle the day with flair,
Fearless souls with fun to spare.
When troubles come, we won't fall,
Just look at this charm, it says it all!

With colors bright and glittered gleam,
It's all a part of our crazy dream.
No worries, friends; just wear a grin,
For courage lies where laughter's been!

So stack them high, let the giggles flow,
Wear your heart; let the world know.
With every jingle, a tale unfolds,
Of brave hearts who just won't be told.

Keepsakes of Courage

Little trinkets on our hands,
Funny faces, wild demands.
Each piece tells a jesting story,
Of silly moments, brave and hoary.

When life throws a curve—oh dear!
Just shake it off, spread the cheer.
With every flick and playful twist,
These trinkets laugh, they can't be missed!

Holding strong through thick and thin,
Where humor's found, we all will win.
So wear these keepsakes, let them swing,
Spread the joy and let hearts sing!

For in their shine, a courage bright,
Dancing shadows with funny light.
These little laughs, a steadfast team,
In the face of fear, we still will dream.

Pendants of the Gallant

Dangle down from necks so bold,
Laughing softly, stories told.
Each pendant has a quirky jest,
In every challenge, we are blessed.

Bravery's charm in a wink of an eye,
With a twist, we all can fly.
Swinging gently, they cheer us on,
In goofy moods, we can't go wrong!

When the going gets tough, keep a smile,
A jiggly pendant can go the mile.
With every jingle, a giggle ensues,
Courage comes dressed in silly hues!

So clasp them tight, let marvels unfold,
These pendants are worth their weight in gold.
With laughter as armor, our spirits ignite,
And even in darkness, we'll shine so bright.

Adornment of the Unbroken

Adorned with patterns, bright and loud,
Each piece stands tall, oh so proud.
Embracing laughs with every clasp,
In wobbly steps, we dare to grasp.

Through wacky times and silly trends,
Our shines remind us, love transcends.
Wear them boldly, what a display,
Making light of life, come what may!

With charms that jiggle and mock the fear,
These adornments bring laughter near.
In every twist, a joke to share,
For unbroken hearts, we're a funny pair!

So let's gather round with all our dreams,
Witty adornments and joyful beams.
With humor as our guide, let's dive,
In the sea of laughter, we will thrive.

Resilience Wrapped in Gold

In a shop of shiny bling,
A warrior bought a thing.
It sparkled like a star,
But it smelled like pickled jar.

Tying knots of silly cheer,
With his charm, he faced the fear.
Each twist a tale of jest,
A laugh became the very best.

He wore it like a crown of pride,
Spreading joy far and wide.
When trouble comes, he simply smiles,
And dances through the trials.

Though life can twist and pull a lot,
His jolly spirit can't be caught.
With jangling laughter, he can cope,
For he is anchored with laughter's rope.

Echoes of the Undaunted

In a land where gators swim,
A hero wore his armor grim.
But his sidekick, quite the clown,
Swapped his gear for a hula gown.

Resilience echoed loud and clear,
As they tackled every fear.
With each step in goofball gear,
They brought a smile, spread some cheer.

Together they faced battles wild,
One tough, the other a child.
They sang and danced through thick and thin,
With goofy grins that'd surely win.

In the fray, they'd shout and squeal,
With laughter as their best appeal.
For the undaunted knew the truth,
Joy was their eternal sleuth.

Charismatic Chains

A chain of laughter, a chain of fun,
Worn by everyone beneath the sun.
It jingled and jangled—what a sound,
A symphony of smiles all around.

With charms of kittens and ice cream cones,
Each link a story, set in tones.
With every step, it sparked delight,
As they twirled and leaped through night.

Dared to wear it to the mall,
Where shoppers turned to laugh and call.
'What's that bling? A fashion scare?'
"Just my armor! Wear it with flair!"

In battles fierce, they'd laugh and play,
Embracing the chaos, come what may.
With charismatic chains that shine,
They taught the world laughter is divine.

Clasped Courage

In a world where courage clips,
One steadfast heart denied the slips.
With clasped charm and vibrant flair,
They laughed at life, quite unaware.

Each clasp a tale of daring pride,
A whiff of mischief by their side.
With a hop, skip, and silly dance,
They took on every wild chance.

"Let's juggle fears like oranges!"
They shouted with face-splitting grins.
Their courage clasped in humor bright,
Turning every fright to sheer delight.

With a twinkle in their eyes so bold,
They conquered fears, like tales of old.
And through the storms, one thing remains,
Their clasped courage, breaking chains.

Celebrating the Unafraid

There once was a lad with a flair,
Who donned bright bands like a dare.
He wore them with pride,
As his friends all cried, 'Hey, where's your fashion affair?'

With colors so bright and so bold,
He told tales of bravery untold.
Every twist and each turn,
Made the onlookers yearn, for that style was pure gold.

He'd dance 'round the town, full of glee,
While the wind played a trick on his knee.
Friends laughed till they cried,
At his dance, so allied, to a tune that was wild and free.

So let's raise a glass to this jest,
For those who wear quirks are the best!
In sparkles and charms,
There's magic that warms, and laughter puts doubt to the
test.

Rivets of Resolve

In the land of the brave, under sun,
Lived a critter who thought it was fun.
With rivets galore,
He barged through the door, shouting, 'Look at this super
cool run!'

With rivets and bolts on his paws,
He strutted with laughter because,
Each clang made a sound,
That echoed around, giving squirrels quite the pause.

His friends tried to match the great style,
But tripped on their own for a while.
With giggles and cheers,
They overcame fears, turning fumbles to fashion so vile.

If you ever feel down and quite low,
Channel that critter in your show.
With flair and some luck,
Just say, 'What the suck!' and let all your colors just glow!

Motifs of the Fearless

There's a lady with flair in her hair,
Who wears all the motifs without care.
Beads glisten and gleam,
She's living the dream, yelling, 'Join me, if you dare!'

Amongst all her friends with no shame,
They'd whisper, 'We're all here for the fame.'
With trinkets a-flying,
High spirits defying, laughter is all we can claim.

In a world where fun makes the rules,
They're the hip-hop brigade, a gang of fools.
With their charms and their laughs,
Forget all the halves, full-hearted, they dance like old
ghouls.

So come, join this troop that is bright,
With motifs galore, let's ignite.
Each charm tells a tale,
No need to be pale, as we twirl through the day and the
night.

Mysteries in Metal

On a quest for her treasure of flair,
A girl found some metal so rare.
With twists and some bends,
She'd fascinate friends, unraveling tales from thin air.

Her arm was a canvas of glee,
It sparkled with secrets, you see.
With every new find,
She'd leave them all blind, guessing what might it be -
whee!

'Is it magic?' they'd ask with delight,
Or a gift from the stars in the night?
With laughter she'd say,
'No, just metal from Clay, but it gives me such joy, what a
sight!'

So wander the world with a grin,
For the mysteries kept deep within.
In each glimmer and flash,
Find the joy in the clash, let your journey of whimsy
begin!

Aura of the Untamed

In the wild, they swing and sway,
Mocking nature, come what may.
Colorful beads, a silly charade,
Dancing like cats in the sun, unafraid.

With glitter that shines, they steal the show,
Elbows bumping when we go toe-to-toe.
Who knew bravery wore such flair?
Wear it with pride, beyond compare!

Laughter rings out, a joyful parade,
When fashion meets guts, don't be dismayed.
These trinkets chat like wild folk,
Shouting adventures, sharing a joke.

So here's to the bold, the funky alliance,
In a world where style meets defiance.
Strut with a grin, let worries flee,
Life's too short for dull accessories!

Legacy of the Unbroken

Legends speak of bravery bold,
But wait—who wore shiny molds?
Spinning tales of courage proud,
With bling that laughs, lively and loud.

Each charm a story, a twist or turn,
Unbreakable spirits, they brightly burn.
In outrageous colors, they claim their place,
With a wink and a nudge, and a cheeky face.

The bold and the quirky take center stage,
Adorned in laughter, they set the gauge.
With every jingle, they dance around,
Encouraging smiles, joy profound.

So here's to the odd, the laughter divine,
A legacy bright, where weirdos shine.
Forget the frowns, reclaim your groove,
Join in the fun—you've nothing to prove!

Courageous Closures

Snap and click, the sound's a cheer,
Like tiny fireworks, bringing good cheer.
They hold the secrets, the giggles we keep,
With each playful lock, our bravery leaps.

Like a whisper in the wind, they'll tease,
An accidental fashion that aims to please.
Turn heads and snicker, let laughter prevail,
Adventures await, as we set sail.

With every clasp, there's a spark of glee,
These colorful metals shout, 'Come play with me!'
Foolishness woven in every thread,
Boldly we march, full steam ahead.

So flaunt your flair, don't shy away,
Courageous closures lead the way.
With a chuckle, we're brave, can't you see?
In this crazy life, just let it be!

Ties of Tenacity

In a world where seriousness reigns,
We find our strength wrapped in chains.
With colors bright, we laugh and cheer,
Each twist a reminder that we persevere.

Like spaghetti noodles, dancing in pots,
Our bonds are silly—giving it lots!
Cling to the moments that sparkle and cheer,
With jangling wonders that conquer our fear.

So tie on your courage, let's create a scene,
With goofy charm, we're a winning team.
Flashing our winks like secrets we share,
In the journey of life, who wouldn't dare?

So here's to the squishy, the oddly entwined,
The ties of tenacity, a promise defined.
With laughter and grit, we'll face what we must,
In whims and in wonders, together we trust!

Echoes in Metal

In a land where heroes dance,
They wear shiny things with a glance.
Jingles and jangles, a merry clang,
Fighting the foes with a silly twang.

A knight in armor, his wrist adorned,
With charms that make all enemies scorned.
"Fear not!" he shouts, as they start to quake,
His bling's so loud, it makes them shake.

Their laughter echoes through the night,
As rings of courage shine so bright.
With every step, a chuckle grows,
Fashion run wild, as courage flows.

Layers of Audacity

Upon the arm, a cascade gleams,
A shimmery layer of wild dreams.
Each trinket holds a daring tale,
Of battles fought, yet never pale.

With rubber ducks and tiny spies,
They brandish smiles, oh so wise!
Defying foes with whimsical grace,
A warrior's pride in a playful space.

A pirate comes, with sparkly chains,
Sends the scallywags running in lanes.
It's not the sword, but the sparkle bold,
That leaves their rivals out in the cold.

Crest of the Fearless

On a crest so bright, the brave do sport,
A funny armory of jesters' court.
With gummy bears and glittered flair,
They stand their ground, without a care.

At the helm, a captain grins with pride,
As unicorns prance by his side.
Foes approach, dismissing their charms,
Then trip and stumble, how laughably disarmed!

With every clash, they giggle and cheer,
Their laughter echoes, loud and clear.
In this colorful war where joy is key,
The fearless brigade dances so free.

Adornment Against Adversity

With every twist, a laugh ignites,
Adornments brightening fierce fights.
A cupcake charm upon their wrist,
Who knew the bold could taste the bliss?

When trouble brews and shadows loom,
They summon strength with a goofy boom.
A clash of wits, as smirks arise,
Fashioning courage in playful guise.

Outrageous baubles, a playful scheme,
Foe-meeting laughter turns fear to steam.
Armored in fun, with style they tread,
For laughter is strength—just look ahead!

Stories Woven with Valor

In a world where courage struts and sways,
We wear our tales like a dazzling craze.
Each twist, each turn, a laughter's roll,
Decorating wrists with a whacky soul.

Proudly flaunting what we dare to share,
A wobbly step, yet we do not care.
Adventures bold, oh what a sight,
In colorful threads, we dance through the night.

Atop a mountain or down in a pit,
Each charm a giggle, each clasp a hit.
Whimsical stories, oh what a mix,
Together we shuffle, throw moves and tricks.

So here's to the days of winks and glee,
In a festival of fun, come laugh with me!
We wear our history, a badge of pride,
In our vibrant bands, let joy be our guide.

Markers of the Intrepid

Oh, the stories that we wear like a crown,
Whimsical markers, we prevent a frown.
In goofy colors, with bling and flair,
Strutting our stuff, in the sun, with care.

Each slap on the wrist is a giggle shared,
Adventures bold with no need to be scared.
From couch to the park, a journey we take,
With laughs that sparkle, oh, make no mistake!

Frogs in bow ties and snakes that can sing,
Our bands tell tales of the joy that we bring.
As we march through life with pep in our step,
We weave in the fun, oh, what a rep!

So gather your friends, let shenanigans flow,
With vibrant markers, let our spirit glow!
Crafting each moment, with laughter and cheer,
In this gallery of glee, we'll shed every fear.

Echoes of Audacity

With every flicker, there's laughter in store,
When we wear our echoes, we're ready to soar.
From silly mishaps to brave little fights,
Our bands are the stories that dance in the lights.

Oh, the echoes we make, like a chorus of fun,
In our vibrant colors, we shine like the sun.
Tales of boldness, with a twist of delight,
Each shimmer of joy sending worries to flight.

"Look at this one!" we giggle and shout,
Each charm a reminder of what life's about.
From kitchen concoctions to pie fights at noon,
Our echoes are silly, they make us balloon!

So let's keep on crafting, with laughter that sticks,
In our bold little bands, let's share all our tricks.
Here's to audacity, wrapped on our wrists,
In the gallery of giggles, it simply exists!

Bands of Bravery

In the circus of life, we juggle our fears,
With bands of silliness, let's toast with cheers!
Each laugh is a victory, each smile a shout,
With colors of courage, we twirl about.

Through ups and downs, we take silly stances,
In the dance of the daring, we all take chances.
Each band a reminder of humor so grand,
With silly surprises that always go hand in hand.

As we prance through the challenges, giggling away,
In our funny little bands, we brighten the day.
From the whispers of courage to roars of delight,
Together we flicker, our spirits ignite!

So gather round, friends, let's twirl with a grin,
In our colorful bands, let the fun times begin!
For moments of bravery wrapped in a jest,
In this joyous parade, we all are blessed!

Guardians of Grit

In a land where courage wears a bling,
Brave hearts dance and sing with a swing.
With wristy armor made for the show,
They face their fears with a glittery glow.

Jesters laugh with courage so loud,
Wearing sparkles, they make us proud.
Fuzzy creatures cheer from a cartoon land,
While warriors strut, so bold and grand.

Tiny charms jingle on each brave wrist,
A blingy shield no one can resist.
A rubber chicken for a knight in plight,
Makes battles fun, not a fearsome fight.

So here's to the brave, with styles divine,
In colorful armor, they brightly shine.
With a wink and a grin, they join the race,
In the land of the fearless, let's all embrace.

Implements of the Unyielding

Quirky gadgets, tough as can be,
Made to help folks feel so free.
One's got a lollipop, oh what fun!
Another's a hammer; let's get this done!

Tools of the brave, all lined in a row,
A silly spatula ready to throw.
You've got the know-how, but don't be a bore,
With laughter and giggles, just open the door.

Gritty and witty, they all come alive,
In this wacky quest, we're ready to strive.
With chocolate syrup, we plot our attack,
Don't underestimate what we have in the backpack!

So equip yourself with a dazzling tool,
Remember to laugh, and play it cool.
In the world of heroes, let humor abound,
With implements of fun, our joy will resound.

Woven Emblems of Valor

Tapes try to stick to a brave lion's mane,
While warriors giggle, not hiding the pain.
Together they weave tales of laughter and cheer,
While jesters dance 'round, for there's nothing to fear.

A unicorn prances with a hula hoop,
While minstrels sing songs of a wacky troop.
Each emblem a story, a shimmer and shine,
They weave through the tales, blurring the line.

Stitched with giggles in colors so bright,
Every warrior laughs in the dead of the night.
With threads of adventure, they bind with delight,
Twirling around in a whimsical flight.

For in all of this fun, what's the moral, you ask?
Embrace the silly; it's not a hard task.
Valor in laughter, a treasure to find,
In this world of comedy, leave worries behind.

Chains from the Heart

Linked together is a bunch of brave pals,
With jingly chains that make silly calls.
A squirrel in armor rides on a bike,
And laughter erupts at each clumsy strike.

With hearts intertwined, they bumble and hop,
Tripping and laughing, they never will stop.
Each heavy link tells a tale of their fun,
Glittering friendship under the sun.

What binds them together? A cupcake, perhaps,
Each silly incident gets great laughs.
With sprinkles and frosting, they carry their pride,
In this chain of giggles, there's nothing to hide.

So here's to the chains, all quirky and bright,
In the kingdom of friendship, we're never uptight.
With laughter as armor, we'll face every start,
Together forever, in chains from the heart.

Aegis of the Unyielding

In a world where courage shines bright,
A wrist of valor, a charming sight.
Adventures await, with laughs and cheer,
Even a tiger's roar might induce a sneer.

Armed with charms that jingle and clink,
Brave souls wear them, while others just think.
They fend off dragons and silly old trolls,
With an attitude fiercer than wild iguana rolls.

These bands of power, oh what a thrill,
They bear the stories, the bold and the ill.
Crafted with laughter and a dash of delight,
No butterfingers here, just the brave taking flight.

So let the style and humor unite,
For laughter and courage both take flight.
Wear them with pride, my fearless friend,
Comedy and valor will never bend.

Wristbands of the Valiant

Roll up your sleeves, it's time for some fun,
With wristbands that sparkle like the morning sun.
They've got the power of a thousand great deeds,
And a joke for each dragon, that's all one needs.

Worn with a grin, amidst battle and jest,
These trinkets of honor are simply the best.
Swinging their charms as they hop all around,
Not heroic deeds, just a twirl on the ground.

Snakes in the grass could lose all their game,
When faced with a warrior who's not one to tame.
He'll tickle their scales, take a brave little stance,
With wristbands that jiggle, they'll join in the dance!

Catch wind of their stories, both funny and bright,
As the world spins around, full of laughter and light.
Valiant and raucous, with mischief galore,
These wristbands are fortresses, tales worth exploring.

Charms of the Dauntless

Upon the wrist lies dauntless grace,
Charms like superstars, in a daring chase.
They ready for battle, or just for a laugh,
As giggles and nectar flow like fine calf.

Jingling with stories of mischief and fun,
These charms illustrate valiance, even for one.
They swagger in tune with the rhythm of play,
Each gesture a laugh, brightening the day.

Adorning the brave, oh what a sight!
Taming the monsters that lurk in the night.
With giggles and charm, they spin tales so grand,
No peril that laughter cannot withstand.

So dance to the tune of these dauntless charms,
Foes may just tremble, and run from their arms.
Wearing a smile, they're ready to fight,
With mischief in tow, and a bounce of delight.

Ornaments of the Bold

Ornaments gleaming, they twinkle and shine,
On wrists of the bold, where courage aligns.
Each bead tells a tale of adventure and flair,
With laughter and pranks that float in the air.

Bold hearts, they laugh at the silliest fears,
With ornaments ringing, the truth's crystal clear.
They make silly faces and dance in the sun,
Every jester joins in, and oh, what fun!

Frogs leap around, thinking they're brave,
While the bold wear their baubles, like jewels from a
cave.
They conquer their doubts with a whimsical song,
And prance through the danger, where the fearless belong.

So dress up those wrists with love and with cheer,
Let bravery blossom, and erase every fear.
In the realm where laughter and courage hold sway,
Ornaments guide them, come what may.

Armor of Dreams

In jest we wear our brightly bands,
To shield from life's rough, slippery hands.
Each charm a laugh, a silly joke,
Worn by warriors, but no need to poke.

With sparkles that dance on crazy days,
They cheer us on in oh-so-funny ways.
A fashion statement, a laugh in the wind,
In this colorful armor, we always win!

We twirl and twist as we strut with flair,
Each jingle and jangle fills the air.
Who knew our style could also be bold?
Turns out laughter never gets old!

So here we stand, our hearts in sync,
With charms that shimmer, simplistic though pink.
For while we stand, we giggle and gleam,
In this wacky world, we're a hilarious team!

Glimmers of Grit

In every sparkle, a story to tell,
Of overcoming battles, yet doing it well.
We wear our bling like proud little knights,
Facing the world with giggles and bites.

The truth is dear, we all need to laugh,
A little bit of grit and a lot of craft.
With jiggly charms that wobble and sway,
We find some joy in the tough day-to-day.

These glimmers of 'you've got this' shine bright,
Reflecting our courage through darkness and light.
Each bead a reminder, we can be bold,
But only if we don't lose our sense of gold!

So let's stack them high, these tokens of cheer,
A protest against the gloomy and drear.
With a wink and a nod, we strut down the lane,
In all our loud colors, we'll dance through the rain!

Heartstrings of Courage

With each little twinkle, we tighten our grip,
On heartstrings of courage, let's take a big skip!
In the face of fears, we chuckle and beam,
With fun little charms, let's chase every dream.

Never mind troubles, we choose to ignore,
A pop of bright colors, who could ask for more?
They laugh as they cling, these pieces of cheer,
A wink to the world, 'we've conquered the fear!'

With rays of sunshine capturing flair,
Our tricky little treasures unwind in the air.
Each giggle we share, a memory we weave,
In hearts full of laughter, we dare to believe!

So let's raise a toast, to wild and free days,
Filled with silly antics and curious ways.
In the tapestry of life, we add our unique spin,
With heartstrings of courage, let the fun begin!

Threads of the Courageous

In threads of bold laughter, we weave our tales,
With softness behind every rugged detail.
Each knot tells a story of strength on display,
With colors that clash in the most charming way.

A tapestry spun from the fabric of dreams,
With giggles and grins bursting at the seams.
We wrap up our worries in wacky delight,
Chasing away shadows, bringing forth light.

So when life gets tough, or it's heavy as lead,
We'll fashion our spirits and dance on ahead.
For each quirky thread adds fun to the scene,
And laughter's the needle, sewing moments unseen!

With quirky designs, and stories galore,
We wear our fierce laughter, who could want more?
In threads of the brave, united we stand,
Spreading the joy across this wild land!

Treasures of Grit

On wrists of warriors, a sparkle so bright,
They wobble and jingle, a comical sight.
Each charm tells a tale of laughter and fight,
Worn by the daring, who dance in the light.

With rubbery bands and a colorful flair,
They twirl like dancers, without a care.
A symbol of strength, or just something rare,
These treasures of grit, in a joyful affair.

Around every bend, they bounce and they cling,
Like kittens on leashes, they bounce and they swing.
Each one a reminder, that all of us sing,
In tune with our giggles, oh, what joy they bring!

With colorful beads and a wild mix of styles,
These trinkets of heart bring us all endless smiles.
So flaunt them with pride, for they hide all the trials,
As we strut down the street, let's go crazy for miles!

Cuffs of the Unbreakable

Oh, these cuffs of courage, they shine with a grin,
For when life gets crazy, let the fun begin!
They jingle and jangle, like a whimsical din,
Crafted with laughter, where victories spin.

With rubber bands stretching, they hold with a laugh,
Like grandma's old stories on a whimsical path.
Through battles and blunders, they chart our own staff,
In the circus of life, they take a bold half.

Each link tells a story, where drawbacks are feats,
Of mishaps in kitchens or sweet, silly treats.
With colors that dazzle, joy simply repeats,
Where cuffs are the power, and laughter completes.

When life tries to tangle, we snap them with cheer,
And shrug off the worry, not a single fear.
For every bold move, there's laughter to steer,
In the cuffs of the brave, we hold what is dear!

Gems of Tenacity

In pockets of laughter, we find them with glee,
These gems of bold spirit, as wild as can be.
With sparkly colors, they shout, 'Come and see!'
Reminders that fighting is simple, you see!

Each gem holds a story, a chuckle or two,
Like mishaps in missions, or tasks overdue.
When life throws confetti, our joy will construe,
As we flaunt these treasures, in vibrant hues too!

They dangle and dangle, like pets on a swing,
Waiting for moments when we laugh and we sing.
In the garden of life, they bloom like spring,
These gems of tenacity, with joy we bring!

A rainbow of hope, every gem takes its place,
Plucked from our struggles, they come with a grace.
In trials we giggle, an awe-inspiring race,
With gems of tenacity, we dance with embrace!

Trinkets of the Bravehearted

Oh, trinkets of fervor, they're cheerful and bright,
Worn by the brave with a wink and a bite.
With every odd bauble, tucked in just right,
They celebrate courage, a comical sight.

These knickknacks of spirit, they jingle with flair,
In moments of laughter, they twirl in the air.
Like whispers of triumph dancing everywhere,
Our hearts lift in joy, with no worry or care.

From quirky to classic, each trinket has flair,
They tell of adventures, in joy we declare.
With all that they carry, they lighten the rare,
Each piece shines with echoes of fun in the air.

So wear them with pride, let the laughter ignite,
For when life gets tough, they make it alright.
In trinkets of heart, we find humor in plight,
In the circus of life, they bring pure delight!

Enchanted Emblems

A charm on my wrist, oh what a delight,
It jangles and jingles, a curious sight.
It brings all the luck, or so I believe,
Just don't ask how many I leave in my sleeve.

With colors so bright, they call me a knight,
In battles of boredom, I'm ready to fight.
Each twinkle and giggle, a boost to my day,
Who knew such baubles could bring so much play?

I've people convinced, I'm a style guru,
But really, who cares if it's polka dot blue?
Worn with a smirk, I strut with such flair,
It's not about fashion, it's just my wild hair!

So here's to the charms, let them dangle and sway,
For laughs and for giggles, they'll brighten my way.
With every sweet clink, I feel like a queen,
In our silly kingdom of sparkle and sheen.

Brilliant Bonds

On my wrist, a party, a joyful parade,
With bands of bright colors, I'm completely arrayed.
They cling to my arm, like good friends would do,
Together we conquer, just us and our crew!

Do people stare? Ah, they can't understand,
These treasures are magic, they brighten the bland.
We laugh at the quirks, like it's perfectly fine,
With every odd jingle, we know we'll shine!

Sometimes they get tangled, oh what a sight,
Like a game of hopscotch, we giggle in spite.
Twists and loops, like our very own dance,
We're like a big family, tucked into one glance!

So here's to the laughter, the joy that we share,
Each clasp holds a memory, crafted with care.
United we sparkle, what a fabulous bond,
In our world of whimsy, I know we're beyond!

Sentinels of the Spirit

Here on my wrist, I have a small crew,
With charms that can cheer me when feelin' blue.
They guard my adventures, my goofy old ways,
With smiles and tickles, they brighten my days.

From unicorns bold to the dragons I flaunt,
These little defenders fill every jaunt.
They're more than just trinkets, they pull up their socks,
In the battles of life, they're my trusty blocks!

When everyone whispers, I just wink and grin,
My warriors sparkle, where shall we begin?
Jokes on the side, oh the fun that we bring,
With laughs like a symphony, hear the joy sing!

So here's my golden armory, get ready to cheer,
For these quirky protectors are always near.
In a world of wild, they keep me in line,
With humor and magic, how lucky I shine!

Wearable Bravery

Oh, what a marvel! These bands that I wear,
With the courage of lions, they banish despair.
They shimmer and dance, what a brave little clan,
Life's trivial battles? Just a wacky plan!

Like fortune cookies, each charm hides a joke,
"Why did the chicken?" if you're ever broke!
We giggle and snicker, a ruckus we make,
With each silly line, we're the laughs that awake!

When gloom dares to linger, just look at my arm,
With the power of friendship, there's no cause for alarm.
These symbols of fun make the mundane sublime,
As we twist through the chaos, we take on our climb!

So here's to the laughter, the joy in the fray,
With every odd jangle, we frolic and play.
Together we laugh, and forever we stand,
In this dazzling quest, my brave little band!

Bands of Defiance

On wrists they twirl, oh what a sight,
With colors bright, they spark delight.
A 'nope' to fate, a wink to cheer,
They dance and jig, when fear is near.

Strapped on like armor, clinks and clanks,
They tell the world, 'We're bold, no pranks!'
With every jingle, a giggle's spread,
Who knew such knots could forge ahead?

With every hue, a story told,
Of battles fought, and hearts of gold.
Around the wrist, they spin and sway,
Laugh at the odds, come what may!

So wear them proud, let spirits rise,
In this mad game, be the surprise!
When life throws shade, make it a show,
With colorful bands, just steal the glow!

Amulets of Endurance

Worn snug and tight, like hugs on call,
They promise, 'Hey! You'll never fall!'
Each charm a laugh, each color a grin,
In this silly life, we always win.

They laugh at clouds, nay! They tease the rain,
With little trinkets, we dance through pain.
Collecting smiles like pearls on chit,
Who knew such laughter could be so fit?

They jingle and jive, like friends at play,
In every color, they dazzle the gray.
So when life's a circus, and you're the clown,
Remember the amulets - wear your crown!

Through ups and downs, they hold us tight,
With twisty tales that ignite delight.
In this wild ride, let each heart sing,
With amulets bold, we conquer everything!

Gems of the Unyielding

Shiny stones on display, oh what a tease,
Each one winks, 'I'll put you at ease!'
In a world of chaos, they gleam and glow,
With sparkles of laughter, they steal the show.

An emerald grins, 'Let's party all night!',
While rubies nod, 'We'll get it right!'
Diamonds chime in with a tiptoe spin,
On this wild ride, let joy begin.

'Wear me for luck, or wear me for fun!'
Said the silly gems, 'Oh, we're never done!'
So stack them high, let the good times roll,
In this bling parade, let laughter console!

Through each little gleam, a riot is sparked,
With playful whispers, they keep us marked.
In this glittered dance, we find our grace,
With gems of the jesters, let's rule the space!

Ornate Oaths

They twist and turn like playful gnomes,
In laughter's grip, they find their homes.
Each intricate loop a promise made,
In this silly game, let joy invade!

A golden swirl says, 'Let's seize the day!'
While silver whispers, 'In jest, let's play!'
They twinkle and bounce, with humor so bright,
Turning mundane into pure delight.

In their bright wraps, bold stories bloom,
Of chortles and chuckles that chase the gloom.
Life's tangled yarn becomes a spree,
In ornate oaths, we all roam free!

So clasp those whims, wear them with pride,
Through winks and giggles, let hearts collide.
With these lovely knots, let's chart our course,
In a merry band where laughter's the force!